INTRODUCTION & CHECKLIST

This guide is intended to introduce the novice to the basics of freshwater fishing including how to fish, where to fish and how to land and prepare your catch. Note that all states have laws governing fishing practices and procedures; it is important to be informed of local rules and regulations before heading out.

Parts of a Fish

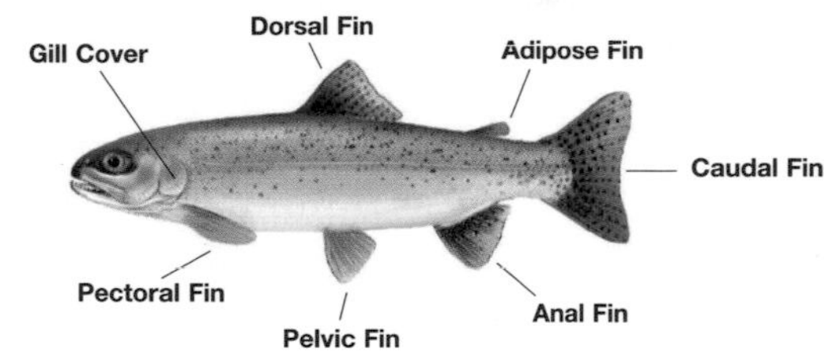

Gill Cover
Dorsal Fin
Adipose Fin
Caudal Fin
Pectoral Fin
Pelvic Fin
Anal Fin

Pre-trip Checklist

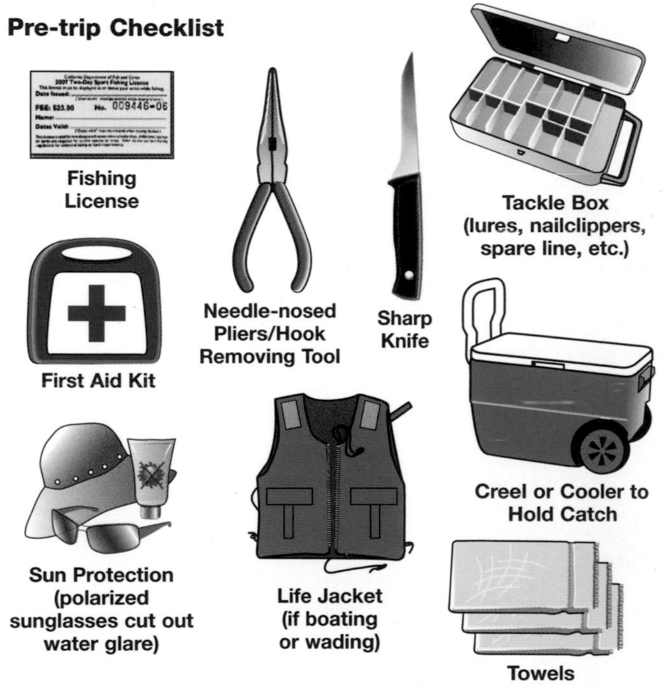

Fishing License
Needle-nosed Pliers/Hook Removing Tool
Sharp Knife
Tackle Box (lures, nailclippers, spare line, etc.)
First Aid Kit
Sun Protection (polarized sunglasses cut out water glare)
Life Jacket (if boating or wading)
Creel or Cooler to Hold Catch
Towels

Most illustrations show the adult male in breeding coloration. Colors and markings may be duller or absent during different seasons. The measurements denote the approximate maximum length of species. Illustrations are not to scale.

Waterford Press publishes reference guides that introduce readers to nature observation, outdoor recreation and survival skills. Product information is featured on the website: **www.waterfordpress.com**

Powerbait® is a registered trademark of Pure Fishing Inc.

ISBN 978-1-58355-535-4

$7.95 U.S
$9.95 CAN.

10 9 8 7 6 5 4 3 2 1   2306508

FRESHWATER FISHING – A Waterproof Folding Guide to What Novices Need to Know

WATERFORD PRESS

A POCKET NATURALIST® GUIDE

FRESHWATER FISHING

A Waterproof Folding Guide to What Novices Need to Know

IT'S THE LAW

Anglers should be aware there are state laws regarding:

- Fishing licenses. **In most states, anglers over the age of 12 MUST purchase a fishing license and have it in their possession.**
- Public access – is fishing allowed in the area?
- Legal baits – can you use live bait or not?
- Approved fishing procedures (e.g., you may not take fish by hand or use explosives or poisons to stun fish).
- Minimum size and bag limits for each species. These will vary in different areas throughout each state.

FISHING BASICS

Before Heading Out

The single most important question to ask yourself before you head out is **what species are you trying to catch?** This will affect the type and size of bait and fishing methods used. Check the size and bag limits and bait restrictions for each species in the area.

Keep It Simple

The contents of many survival kits reveal the inherent simplicity of fishing – they contain some hooks and line. Tie the line to a hook, bait the hook and you are ready to fish.

The simplest way to begin to learn how to fish is to buy an inexpensive all-in-one kit that includes a rod, a reel with line, some hooks and artificial lures.

Basic Casting – Push-Button Rod & Reel

The simplest reel to operate is a push-button (spincasting) reel.

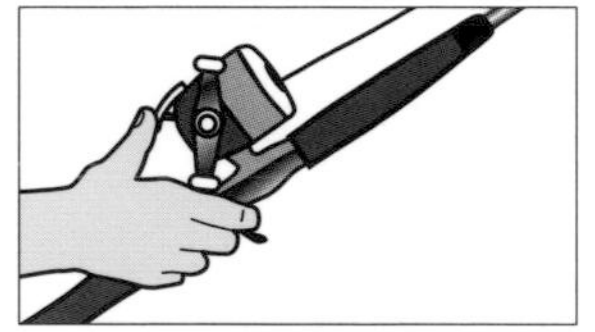

1. Depress button on reel and hold down.

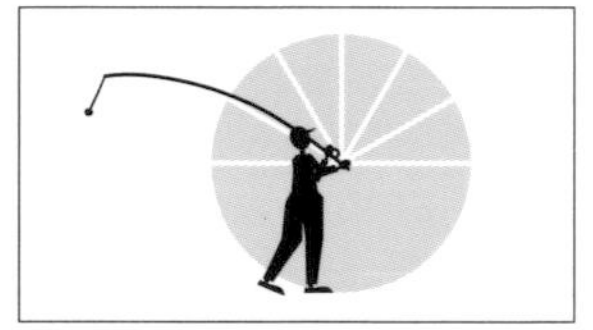

2. Pull back rod to 10 o'clock.

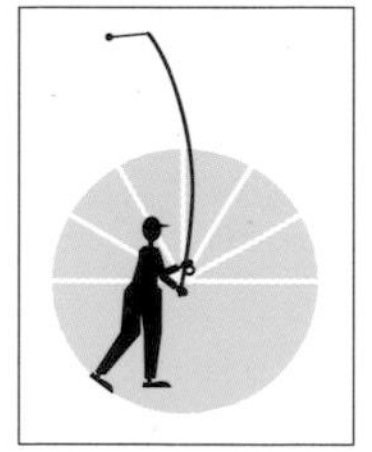

3. Bring rod forward. **Release button at 12 o'clock** to release line and bait.

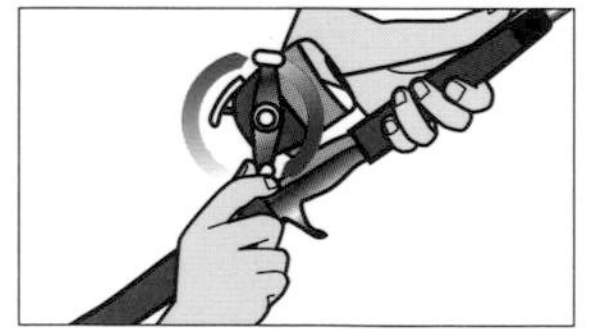

4. After bait is cast, engage line retrieve by cranking on reel handle.

GENERAL FISHING SAFETY

- When casting, look behind you before casting.
- NEVER grab a fish near the hook.
- Remove hooks from fish with needle-nose pliers.
- Wear a life jacket (personal floatation device – PFD) on boats.
- Never wade into unknown water; wear your PFD when wading.

FISHING BASICS

Line & Hooks

Lines are available in a variety of strengths referred to as 'pound test'. The pound test is a general indication of how much force it will take to break the line. For novice anglers, the most common lines used are 6-10 lb. test lines.

To attach a line to any bait or rig, use an easy and strong knot like the Palomar knot. The size of hook/bait you attach will depend on the type of fish you are trying to catch. See back panels for species-specific information on recommended hook size.

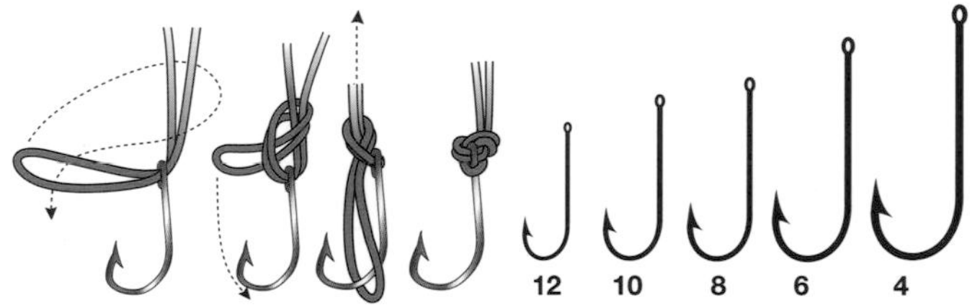

12
10
8
6
4

Palomar Knot   Hooks Shown Actual Size

Bait

Natural bait is usually preferred by anglers since it is more effective. Always check to ensure it is legal to fish with live bait in your area.

NATURAL BAIT

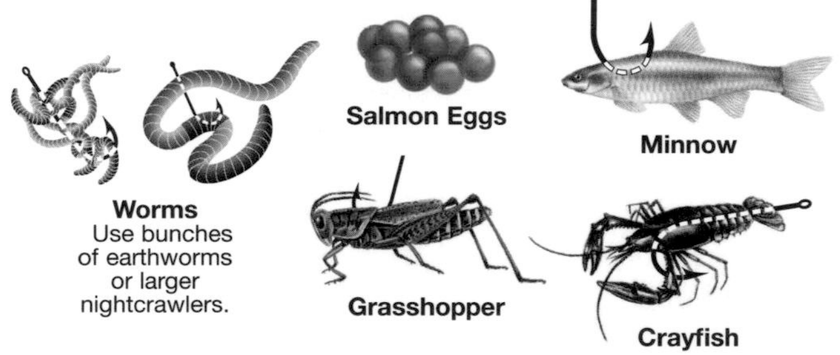

Worms
Use bunches of earthworms or larger nightcrawlers.
Salmon Eggs
Minnow
Grasshopper
Crayfish

ARTIFICIAL BAIT

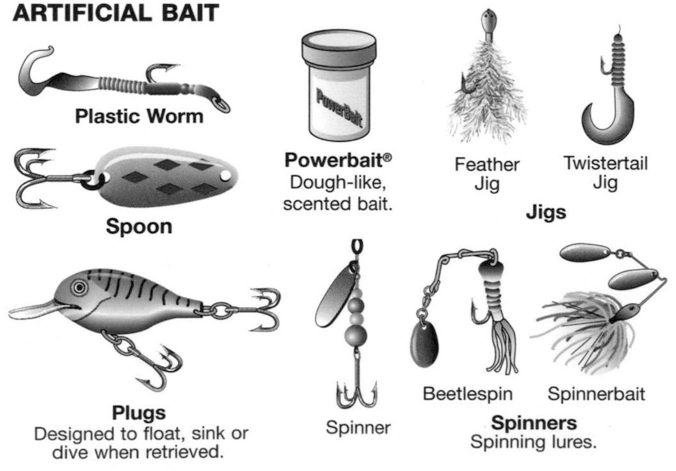

Plastic Worm
Spoon
Powerbait®
Dough-like, scented bait.
Feather Jig
Twistertail Jig
Jigs
Plugs
Designed to float, sink or dive when retrieved.
Spinner
Beetlespin
Spinnerbait
Spinners
Spinning lures.

FISHING BASICS

Rigging a Bait & Fishing Methods

A rigged bait can range from a worm on a hook to complicated arrangements of sinkers, swivels and leaders used to present the bait to the fish in the ideal manner.

RIGGING ACCESSORIES

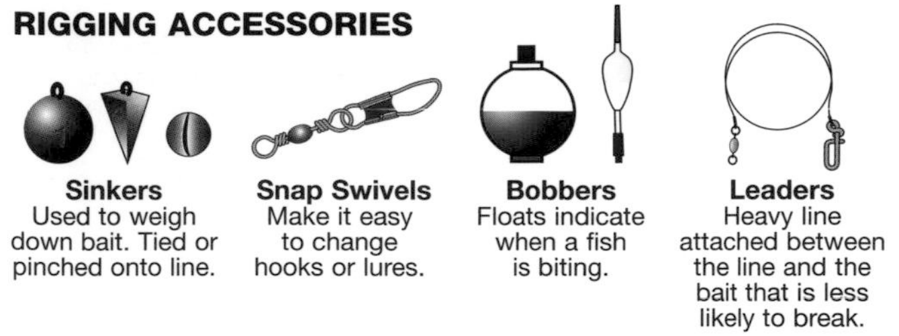

Sinkers
Used to weigh down bait. Tied or pinched onto line.
Snap Swivels
Make it easy to change hooks or lures.
Bobbers
Floats indicate when a fish is biting.
Leaders
Heavy line attached between the line and the bait that is less likely to break.

BOBBER BAIT RIG & FISHING METHOD

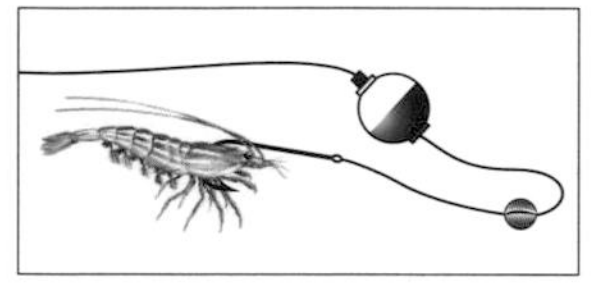

Bobber rig with sinker and bait.

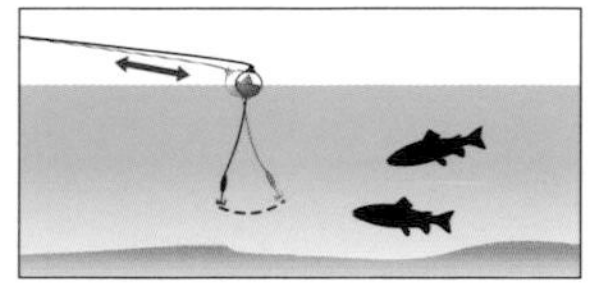

Keep line tight. Twitch line every 10-20 seconds to move the bait.

SPINNING METHODS

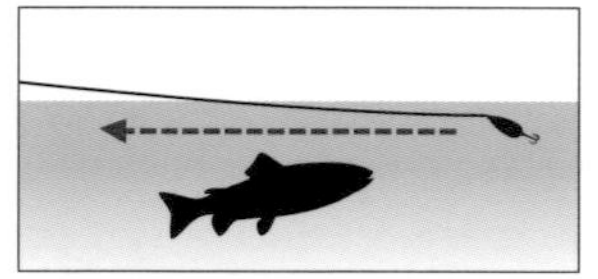

When fishing large spinners, retrieve FAST so it bounces over the surface.

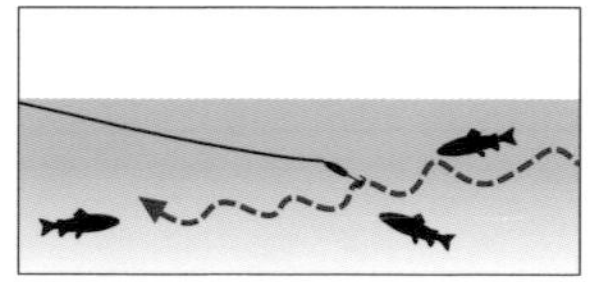

Twitch line every few seconds while retrieving. Keep bait at a constant depth.

JIGGING RIG & FISHING METHOD

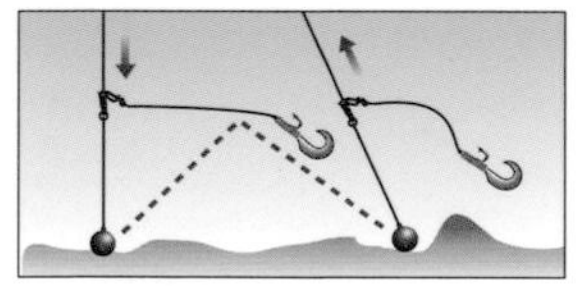

Let sinker hit bottom. Lift rod tip slightly to move jig. Reel in slack and repeat.

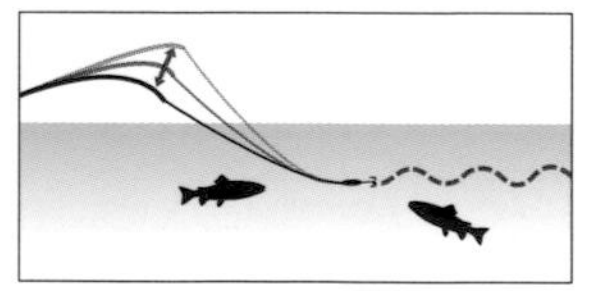

If fish are not near the bottom, use a similar retrieve action to 'swim' the jig.

BOTTOM BAIT FISHING METHOD

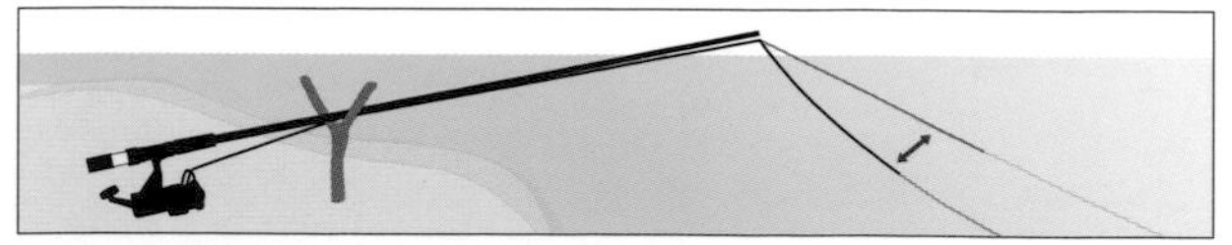

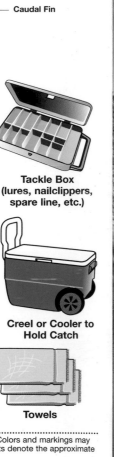

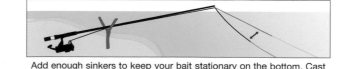

Add enough sinkers to keep your bait stationary on the bottom. Cast it where you think the fish are and let them come to your bait. If fish don't bite, cast to new spot every 15-20 minutes. While waiting for a bite, prop your rod on a Y-stick and wait for the line to twitch.

CATCH A FISH

Do You Have a Bite?

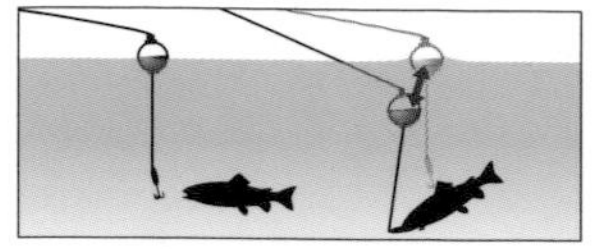

Bobbers Bites
Bobber will twitch or start to travel.

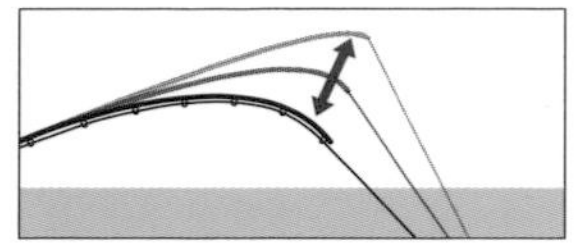

Jig & Bottom Rig Bites
When line twitches or jumps, you have a bite.

3 STEPS TO CATCH AND LAND A FISH

STEP 1 – SET THE HOOK

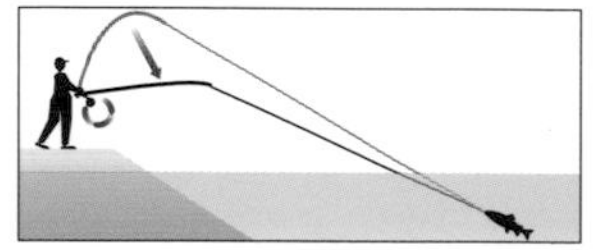

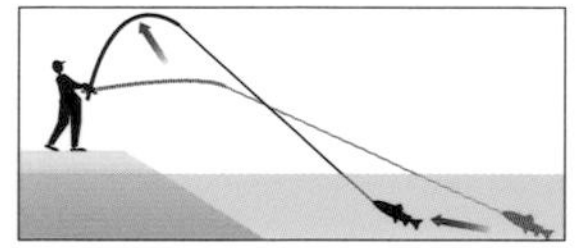

Once you have a bite, set the hook quickly (within 5 seconds). When you feel a fish biting, move the rod to 3 o'clock and reel in excess line. Quickly pull the rod to 1 o'clock to set the hook. How hard you set the hook depends on the species you are trying to catch. Small fish (esp. crappies) have delicate mouths and you can tear the hook out of their mouth if you set it too hard.

STEP 2 – REEL IN THE FISH

Once the hook is set, let the fish make the first move and feel how hard it can pull. If it pulls hard, let it; **NEVER** reel in line when a fish is pulling since this may cause the line to snap. **Increase the drag* on your line** if the fish is pulling out a lot of line quickly. Once the fish tires and stops pulling hard, slowly lower your rod tip to 3 o'clock and start reeling it in, raising your rod tip at the same time to keep tension on the line. **ALWAYS keep tension on the line (a bend in the rod) to keep the hook set while reeling in.** Repeat this motion until the fish is nearby and ready to land.

* 'Drag' varies the tension on the line and speed at which it is released from the reel. A dial on the reel adjusts the drag. Drag should be pre-set according to pound-strength ('test') of your line.

STEP 3 – LAND THE FISH

Note: Always wet your hand before contacting a fish to avoid disturbing its protective slime layer.

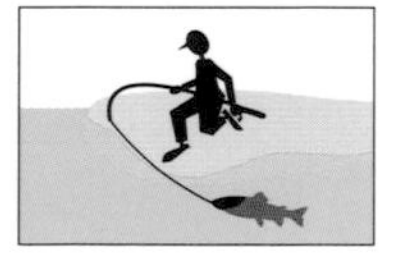

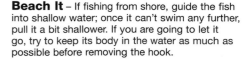

Beach It – If fishing from shore, guide the fish into shallow water; once it can't swim any further, pull it a bit shallower. If you are going to let it go, try to keep its body in the water as much as possible before removing the hook.

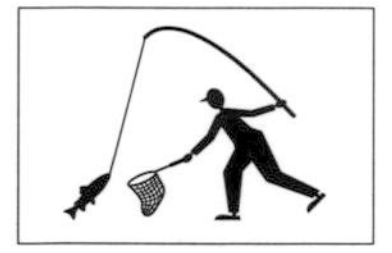

Net It – Lead the fish into the net headfirst so if it tries to run at the last minute, it runs into the net. If releasing the fish, keep the net and the fish in the water as you unhook it.

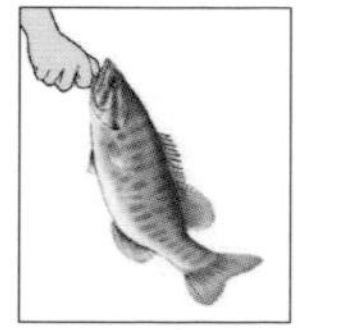

Grab It – For bass, panfish and other toothless fish, wet your hand and grab it by the top or bottom lip with your thumb and index finger. Watch out for the hook!

Think Like a Fish
To know how to catch fish it helps to "think like a fish." Good anglers understand the habits of fish, their senses, tendencies and how and where they like to feed.

See Like a Fish
Fish are easily spooked and will scatter when they spot surface movements. Water bends light and fish can see a lot more of the shore than you think. Always try to avoid casting shadows on the surface. If you see fish in the water, always approach from the downstream side.

When to Fish
As a rule, fish usually feed just before dawn, just after dusk and just before storms. Fish are often feeding when there is abundant insect activity on the surface; they'll indicate their presence by splashing or creating surface ripples. Jumping minnows also indicate feeding fish.

Where to Fish
Fish prefer to live where the water temperature is most comfortable. In lakes and rivers, they often move to deeper, cooler waters when it is hot out. They will return to the shallow shoreside waters to feed at dawn and dusk.

STREAMS & RIVERS

① **Tributaries/Waterfalls** – Fish often congregate and feed at the base of falls or the inlets of feeder streams.
② **Eddies** – Where water swirls around an object to create calm areas.
③ **Riffles** – Stretches of turbulent shallow water over rocks.
④ **Deadfalls, Boulders** – Any object that obstructs current is a place where fish lay in wait for food.
⑤ **Shallow Weed Beds** – Many fish such as pike and bass prefer to hunt in weed-choked waters.
⑥ **Holes** – The outside of bends and the head of deep pools often have deep holes where fish rest.

PONDS & LAKES

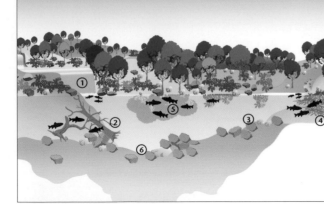

① **Inlets & Outlets** – Fish congregate where water enters or leaves a lake.
② **Underwater Cover** – Fallen trees, brush piles and dock pilings are a favorite habitat of bass and crappies.
③ **Rocky Points** – These areas often divert water current and provide calm waters for fish to feed in.
④ **Weed Beds** – A sanctuary for bait fish, these areas also attract their predators.
⑤ **Shade** – Bankside trees and lily pads provide shade that protects game fish from their predators.
⑥ **Drop-offs** – In areas where water suddenly increases in depth, fish will congregate in the downstream side of the drop-off.

SUNFISH

These small fish are very common and fun for kids to catch. Short and skinny, they often hide in weeds to avoid predators.

Where: Lakes, ponds, waterways.
When: All day.
Bait: *Artificial* = jigs, beetle spins.
Live = small worms, tiny minnows to 1 in. (3 cm), grubs, crayfish.
Tackle: Line = 4 lb.;
Hook size =10.
Method: Bobbing, spinning, jigging.

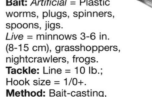

Bluegill
Lepomis macrochirus
To 16 in. (40 cm)
Weight = .5-4.7 lbs.
(.2-2.2 kg)

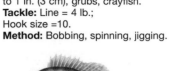

Redear Sunfish
Lepomis microlophus
To 14 in. (35 cm)
Has red spot near dark ear flap.
Weight = .5-5.7 lbs. (.2-2.6 kg)

Pumpkinseed
Lepomis gibbosus
To 16 in. (40 cm)
Weight = .4-1.5 lbs. (.2-.6 kg)

CRAPPIE

Often found in the company of sunfish, crappies have larger mouths and black-and-white speckled sides.

Where: Clear, weedy lakes and ponds.
When: All day.
Bait: *Artificial* = jigs, beetle spins, spoons.
Live = small minnows, grubs.
Tackle: Line = 4 lb.;
Hook size = 6.
Method: Bobbing, spinning.
Notes: Also called 'papermouths' for the thin skin surrounding the mouth.

Black Crappie
Pomoxis nigromaculatus
To 16 in. (40 cm)
Has a humped back and 7-8 dorsal spines.
Weight = .5-5 lbs. (.2-2.3 kg)

BASS

Some of the most popular sport fish, they are known for making spectacular jumps when trying to throw the hook.

Largemouth Bass
Where: Prefer weedy lakes and slow streams/rivers.
When: Dawn and dusk.
Bait: *Artificial* = Plastic worms, plugs, spinners, spoons, jigs.
Live = minnows 3-6 in. (8-15 cm), grasshoppers, nightcrawlers, frogs.
Tackle: Line = 10 lb.;
Hook size = 1/0+.
Method: Bait-casting, spinning, bottom fishing.
Notes: Hangs around sources of cover like logs, weeds, brush and docks. Loves to take spinnerbaits cranked quickly over weedy areas.

Largemouth Bass
Micropterus salmoides To 38 in. (95 cm)
Jaw joint extends beyond the eye.
Note long dark side stripe.
Weight = 1-22.3 lbs. (.4-10 kg)

Smallmouth Bass
Where: Prefer cool, clear streams/rivers and lakes.
When: All day.
Bait: *Artificial* = jigs, spinners, flies.
Live = minnows 2-4 in. (5-10 cm), crayfish, worms.
Tackle: Line = 6 lb.;
Hook size = 1+.
Method: Bait-casting, spinning, bottom fishing.

Smallmouth Bass
Micropterus dolomieu To 27 in. (68 cm)
Jaw joint is beneath the eye. Note barred sides. Weight = 1-12 lbs. (.5-5.4 kg)

Rock Bass
Where: Cool streams, shallow lakes with weedy cover.
When: All day.
Bait: *Artificial* = jigs, spinners, flies.
Live = almost anything goes.
Tackle: Line = 4 lb.;
Hook size = 4.
Method: Bobbing, spinning.

Rock Bass
Ambloplites rupestris To 17 in. (43 cm)
Note red eyes and side blotches.
Weight = .5-3 lbs. (.2-1.3 kg)

TROUT

Rainbow Trout
Where: Streams, rivers, lakes.
When: All day.
Bait: *Artificial* = jigs, spinners, flies, spoons in lakes, Powerbait®.
Live = worms, salmon eggs, minnows 2-3 in. (5-8 cm), grasshoppers.
Tackle: Line = 4 lb.;
Hook size = 12-6.
Method: Spinning, jigging.

Rainbow Trout
Oncorhynchus mykiss
To 44 lb. (1.1 m)
Note spotted body and pinkish side stripe.
Weight = 1-48 lbs. (.4-22 kg)

PIKE

Northern Pike
Where: Shallow waters in weedy lakes and rivers.
When: All day.
Bait: *Artificial* = Spoons, spinners, plugs.
Live = anything goes, minnows 4-8 in. (10-20 cm), small perch.
Tackle: Line = 12 lb.;
Hook size = 1/0+.
Method: Spinning, bottom fishing.
Notes: Loves to take spinnerbaits and spoons cranked quickly over weedy areas.

Northern Pike
Esox lucius
To 53 in. (1.4 m)
Note large head and posterior dorsal fin.
Weight = 1-55 lbs. (.4-25 kg)

PERCH & WALLEYE

Yellow Perch
Where: Lakes, ponds, tidal rivers, lazy streams.
When: All day.
Bait: *Artificial* = jigs, spinners, flies, spoons.
Live = worms, small minnows, crickets, grasshoppers.
Tackle: Line = 4 lb.;
Hook size = 8.
Method: Bottom fishing, jigging, spinning or bobbing.

Yellow Perch
Perca flavescens To 16 in. (40 cm)
Note 6-9 dark 'saddles' down its side.
Weight = 1-4 lbs. (.4-1.9 kg)

Walleye
Where: Clear rivers and lakes.
When: Best at night.
Bait: *Artificial* = jigs, spinners, plugs, flies.
Live = leeches, nightcrawlers, minnows 2-4 in. (5-10 cm), small lampreys.
Tackle: Line = 6 lb.;
Hook size = 2.
Method: Bottom fishing, jigging, bobbing.

Walleye
Sander vitreus To 40 in. (1 m)
Note dark spot on rear of first dorsal fin.
Weight = 1-25 lbs. (.4-11 kg)

BOTTOM FISH

These fish feed along the bottoms of lakes and waterways and are easily identified by their long whiskers (called barbels) which they use to sense the presence of prey.

Catfish
Where: Clear, slow rivers, mud-bottomed lakes.
When: Generally best at night.
Bait: *Artificial* = jigs, spinners, spoons, doughballs, stinkbait.
Live = minnows 2-8 in. (5-20 cm) alive or dead, frogs, crayfish.
Tackle: Line = 10 lb.;
Hook size = 1/0+.
Method: Bottom fishing.
Notes: Specially prepared stinkbaits of rotten chicken guts, cheese and dried blood work well.

Channel Catfish
Ictalurus punctatus To 4 ft. (1.2 m)
Note black-spotted sides and rounded anal fin. Weight = 1-58 lbs. (.4-26 kg)

Bullhead
Where: Deep lakes, warm ponds, slow-moving streams.
When: All day.
Bait: *Artificial* = jigs, spinners, flies, doughballs, stinkbait.
Live = worms, snails, leeches, crickets.
Tackle: Line = 4 lb.;
Hook size = 2.
Method: Bottom fishing.

Brown Bullhead
Ameiurus nebulosus To 19 in. (48 cm)
Brown above, white below with mottled sides. Weight = .5-7.4 lbs. (.2-3.3 kg)

Carp
Where: Lakes, ponds
When: All day.
Bait: *Artificial* = jigs, flies, doughballs.
Live = nightcrawlers.
Tackle: Line = 8 lb.; Hook size = 1.
Method: Bottom fishing.
Notes: Widely introduced non-native species.

Common Carp
Cyprinus carpio To 36 in. (90 cm)
Note arched back, mouth barbels and orangish fins.
Weight = 1-75.8 lbs. (.4-34.4 kg)

Is It a Keeper?
First measure the fish from nose to tail tip to ensure it meets the minimum size requirement. If it is too small, release it.

Catch & Release
1. Keep the fish in the water and handle it as little as possible. Ensure your hands are wet.
2. If the fish lacks teeth, grab its lower jaw with your thumb and index finger. If the fish has teeth, grasp it across the back of the head.
3. Using needlenose pliers or a fishhook remover, attempt to free the hook. If the hook is too deep or cannot be easily removed, simply cut the line. The hook will eventually dissolve or come loose.
4. If the fish is played-out, revive it by holding its head forward in the current or moving it through the water slowly.

How to Humanely Kill a Fish
Using a heavy, blunt object, hit down sharply on the head behind the eyes. For harder to kill species like catfish, insert knife tip at forward end of spine; push down to sever spinal cord.

Filleting a Fish
The following shows a simple method to fillet (remove the flesh from) a fish.

1. Cut behind the pectoral fin on an angle.

2. Run the knife along one side of the backbone.

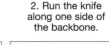

3. Run the knife down the side along the rib down to the tail.

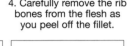

4. Carefully remove the rib bones from the flesh as you peel off the fillet.

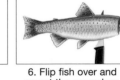

5. Remove the skin from the flesh.

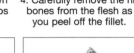

6. Flip fish over and repeat the procedure.

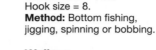